CHASING HAPPINESS

ANKIT BALWADA

To my parents who love me enough to let me fly. ♥

This book is a tribute to the legacy of my late great-grandfather and freedom fighter, *Choudhary Tara Chand Ji Jharoda*—whose hard life and relentless struggles played a crucial role in securing India's freedom, where I can write freely about anything.

I dedicate this book to all young guns eager to make meaningful contributions to society.

A reminder that life is priceless. Do Hustle often!

Contents

Acknowledgements

I cannot possibly thank everyone who has contributed to this book. Every person who came into my life in my amazing 20s has played a part. To all the amazing young folks I met during my solo travels with whom we shared dorm beds, rental scooters, food, drinks, wild parties, adventures, late-night talks, tears, laughter and much more. The different energies I have experienced over the last decade have pretty much changed the way I look at life. Yet ecstatically these moments have evoked certain wisdom in me which constantly remind me of the beauty and uncertainty of life. Priceless!

There are many wonderful people I would like to thank for supporting me in writing this book.

My MamaJi Adv. Kulbhan Punia, has always been special to me and always supported me no matter what the situation is and encouraged me to chase my dreams.

My parents, for inculcating in me the right habits and choices in life. Thank you for this life, your blessings, your strength and much more

My family and friends that surrounds me, love me and make life fun.

Last, but not least, I would like to express my gratitude to all the readers, who bought my book. Hope you find it worthy of your time. Cheers!

Preface

As I celebrate my 30th birthday, I find myself at a unique crossroads—a time when the awareness of our finite journey becomes both a gentle reminder and a compelling call to live more authentically. This book was born from that very moment of reflection. I asked myself, *"What would I tell my younger self, just stepping into the whirlwind of the 20s?"* The answer was clear: share the real, raw journey of chasing happiness, with all its ups, downs and unexpected turns.

For years, I have been chronicling my experiences—those exhilarating highs and lows of my professional career, building a bootstrapped startup, actively volunteering for social causes and nurturing a loving family, intertwined with the quieter, more challenging moments of self-doubt, setbacks and the struggle to find the true meaning of life.

From professional blunders and rejections to personal setbacks and unexpected injuries, I learned that life is less like a perfectly coded program and more like a chaotic and unpredictable journey, where rebooting isn't always a matter of a quick fix. Often, when things do not unfold as planned, I am reminded that I must start over from scratch to continue playing this endless game of life. I work hard to maintain a calm mindset and navigate through the challenges, pushing myself each day to rise above the turmoil and confront the world with steadfast confidence. In these moments, the setbacks—whether in personal realms or professional endeavors—create a void within us that most often goes unnoticed by those around us.

Even though I have frequently been seen as the ever-positive force, ever-ready to take on whatever comes my way, there have been times when deep-seated insecurities and unspoken failures have weighed me down. *Isn't it interesting how people think of themselves because it is often not how other people think of them?*

In these pages, you will find a collection of insights and real-life incidents from today's 20-something youth—a period that is as enlightening as it is humbling. I will share stories of both triumphs and tribulations, hoping to illuminate the truth that our paths are as unique as our individual struggles. This is not just a celebration of success; it is an honest exploration of the spaces in between—the moments of vulnerability that ultimately pave the way for genuine growth. It took a lot of courage to be able to put my life out there and bring these stories to the world.

Expect to encounter lessons on resilience, the power of retrospection and the importance of sitting with someone in their darkest moments rather than rushing to offer unsolicited advice. I hope my journey reminds you that it's okay not to have everything figured out. Life, with all its unpredictable twists, is about chasing happiness in our own way, embracing imperfections and learning to rise after every fall.

Thank you for joining me on this reflective voyage. May these pages offer you comfort, clarity and the courage to forge your own path—no matter how uncertain it may seem.

CHAPTER ONE

Gratitude

I would like to begin this book by talking about one of the most powerful and inexpensive tools available on this planet – **Gratitude**. It invites us to appreciate what we have, irrespective of whether tangible or intangible, rather than focusing on what we lack or chasing after new things in the hope of finding happiness.

Moreover, by acknowledging the goodness in our lives, we come to realize that these blessings often originate from outside ourselves—through the kindness of others, the beauty of nature, or the influence of a higher power. In doing so, gratitude connects us to something much larger than our individual existence.

In psychology, gratitude is strongly linked to happiness as it helps boost positive emotions, allows us to savor good experiences, improves our health, helps us cope with adversity, and fosters stronger relationships. You can always find ways to have gratitude for all that you have and all that you are. Spend less time counting calories and more time counting your blessings Avoid comparing yourself to others or molding your actions to fit their expectations—doing so will only lead to misery. Stay true to yourself and strive to become the person you were meant to be. Each day is an opportunity, feel grateful for the little things in your life and remember that it is the sum of small things that make up the bigger beautiful picture of happiness.

So if I am chasing happiness, has my definition of success and achievement changed?

In many ways, yes. Achievement matters because it builds momentum—a series of small wins rather than static, absolute milestones—which often fosters a genuine sense of success. As humans, we're wired to appreciate tangible progress. We naturally seek out milestones and metrics, and there's nothing wrong with that, provided we don't let them entirely define our fulfillment.

It's entirely possible to hit impressive targets and yet not feel truly successful. We've seen people who have achieved extraordinary feats but still struggle to find happiness, continuously pushing themselves in search of that elusive sense of accomplishment. Conversely, some individuals, despite not ticking all the conventional boxes of achievement by Western standards, feel deeply successful and content.

Renowned basketball coach John Wooden encapsulated this idea perfectly by defining success as being the best version of yourself and losing isn't a mark of failure—it highlights the joy in the process of trying and improving, rather than merely winning. When we pursue something with unwavering passion and refuse to give up, even setbacks and criticism can become enriching parts of the journey. Ultimately, the pursuit of happiness is rooted in a deep sense of gratitude for the life we live.

How to discover your Why?

It's the core of who you are, not something externally imposed, shaped by your upbringing and experiences. Your "why" resides deep within and if you are fortunate enough to go on the journey of self-discovery and if you can articulate what truly drives you—then most probably you will figure out the gut instinct, purpose or belief that motivates you.

Very often, it's during the struggles and the moments when you feel you have hit rock bottom that you realize your true purpose. There's always a tipping point that arrives when you start filtering out the noise of everyday life and start focusing instead on what are essentials. When you shift the conversation from the distractions to your core beliefs during those pivotal moments, everything changes and your "why" becomes clear.

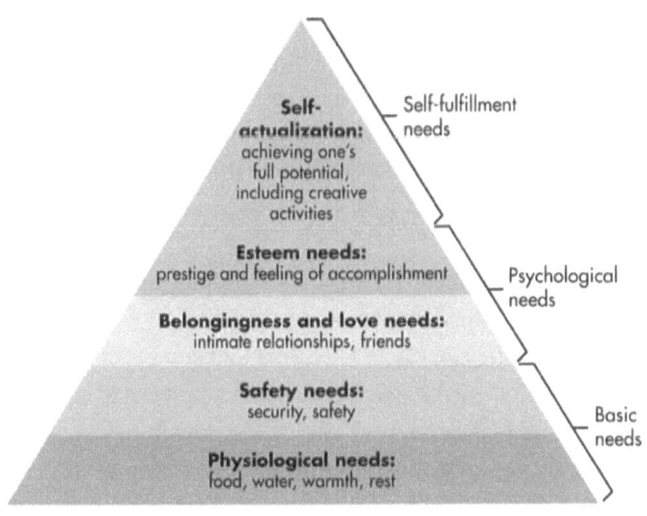

Maslow's Hierarchy of Needs

"Swadharm" self-actualization

Maslow's Hierarchy of Needs offers a modern roadmap that beautifully parallels our personal journeys. At the foundation, we have our basic necessities—food, water and shelter—essential for mere survival. Once these are secured, our focus naturally shifts to safety and security. From there, the need for connection and belonging emerges, much like the rediscovery of friendships and personal relationships as we mature. Building on that, we seek esteem—a blend of self-respect and the recognition we receive from others—which eventually leads us to the pinnacle of the pyramid: self-actualization, the realization of our full potential.

On similar ground, in our 20s the pursuit of a stable and secure career often takes center stage, causing many to temporarily sideline friendships and personal connections. Once professional stability is achieved, the realization emerges that relationships—love, companionship and genuine friendship—are essential to our well-being. This phase then naturally gives way to the quest for respect and social status, milestones that unfold at their own pace, though some people even could not experience them in their lifetime.

Ultimately, this journey is about reaching self-actualization: discovering and living out one's true potential. In the Bhagavad Gita, this journey is encapsulated by the term "Swadharm," a Sanskrit concept that refers to an individual's inherent duties, responsibilities and the pursuit of righteousness. It reminds us that aligning our actions with our natural disposition, talents and passions is the key to leading a balanced and meaningful life. It encourages you to embrace actions and follow the path that:

- align with your nature, true abilities and inner calling.
- feel naturally compelled to pursue.
- uplift your spirit and contribute to your personal growth.
- comes most naturally to you, letting your true self guide your decisions.

The benefits of living in accordance with your Swadharm are significant. By staying true to your inner calling, you are leading to a life that is not only purposeful but also deeply rewarding. Life itself is a gift and the essence of a gift is that it is meant to be shared. If you possess talents, wisdom or abilities but choose to keep them to yourself, you are withholding something valuable from the world. True fulfillment comes when you share your gifts with others, using them to uplift, inspire and make a positive difference.

CHAPTER TWO

Mental Health: A Call for a Holistic Approach

Mental health is one of today's most controversial and underrated topics. Traditional overtly medicalized approaches often focus solely on diagnosis, prognosis and intervention, overlooking the broader structural determinants that impact our well-being. In our fast-paced, high-pressure society, additional stressors—like an overwhelming work-life balance—play a crucial role in mental health, yet they are frequently ignored by conventional methods.

I remember one lazy afternoon at home when I watched my mother busily engaged in household chores, assisted by my loving aunt (Maasi). I was enjoying their warm sisterly conversations from a distance as they tackled the herculean task of cleaning a ton of wheat in a single day. During a break, I offered them water and hot masala tea—a simple act I call **"Jal Seva"**. Amid their lighthearted conversation, my mother casually remarked, "Don't you think today's youth are too fragile? They complain about tension or depression over minor issues. They do not have that many responsibilities and the hardships we faced in our times". My aunt agreed, dismissing such concerns as mere theatrics; after all, why would someone claim depression if they weren't really suffering?

I could not help but challenge their perspective: "How can you compare such extremes? If someone is genuinely struggling with mental health, why would there be tangible signs—much like a physical illness shows symptoms like a fever?" My words seemed to catch them off guard as if they were totally unaware of this simple logic. Pausing their work, they looked at me with genuine curiosity and asked, "Then how can we truly recognize if someone is facing mental health issues?"

I calmly explained that the key lies in empathy and close observation. Gave an analogy that just like a doctor relies on biological readings to assess physical health, those around us can often detect when something is amiss by truly understanding a person's way of living. Engaging in open, heartfelt conversations and paying attention to subtle changes in behavior can be as valuable as any clinical test. A robust support system—whether family, a partner or close friends—often serves as the best safeguard. Individuals who have endured tough times are more likely to appreciate the true value of such support. And if such support is not already in place, it is essential to work towards building these meaningful connections. Humans are inherently social creatures and having a supportive network can make navigating life's challenges much easier.

My own journey reinforces this perspective. There was a time when I spent all my energy pretending to be happy, successful and in control—masking the deep struggles within me. I became so adept at hiding my true state that even my family failed to notice. It wasn't until a dear friend pointed out that something was wrong that I recognized the toll of living a lie. That intervention became a turning point, redirecting my energy from hiding my pain to rediscovering my passion. I came out of the loophole that I was sinking in, as this shift allowed me to make bold, life-changing decisions with newfound confidence.

Ultimately, understanding another person's mental health struggles can be profoundly challenging unless one has experienced similar hardships. It is through shared experiences and empathetic listening that we can begin to bridge the gap between mere observation and genuine understanding. I would like to illustrate some personal experiences involving mental health.

Early 20s: Involving two close friends

Lesson: Approach other's POV with empathy and insight

Shrey's Story:

Shrey, who comes from a comfortable middle-class background, struggled to secure a government job—a notoriously competitive arena in India where one vacancy can attract lakhs of applicants. Despite his intelligence and hard work, every exam he took ended in disappointment. Even the brightest minds often find it challenging to clear these exams successfully. The consistently high rejection rate undoubtedly takes a toll on those who attempt these tests, especially when you add the additional pressure from parents and society that cannot be ignored. He was a studious and intelligent individual, yet from the end of our graduation through the first few years thereafter, I witnessed him struggle profoundly with mental health—an experience that I found difficult to fully relate to, even though I had faced similar academic setbacks myself.

I also prepared to crack one of the toughest exams in the world- IIT JEE in the Kota factory of students. I dedicated three years -11th, 12th and a drop year to this pursuit, yet I fell short of joining the prestigious IITs. During that challenging period, the support and guidance of my parents helped me recover, even as I faced the daunting transition into college life. It felt as though the world had come crashing down on me during that period. However, during that challenging period, my parents held my hand and guided me. Yet, as soon as I entered my first year of college, I seemed to forget all those hardships and found myself lost in a vibrant, seemingly cheerful world that I had never encountered before.

Kitty's Breakup:

On the other hand, Kitty went through a very bad breakup in her first relationship that plunged her into a deep depression lasting nearly a year and a half. Despite their closeness as my very good friends, I struggled to connect with either of their situations. The simple reason was that I had never ever faced mental health issues. At that time, I was in a very beautiful and stable phase in my life and had already secured a position at a multinational company with a handsome paycheck. Consequently, when I attempted to discuss their issues with them, my comments came across as unempathetic and dismissive, "You both are so weak—why can't you just shrug off these setbacks? It's normal to get hurt or stumble in life". In hindsight, with my straightforward words, I was not helping them but making a monkey out of them. I now recognize how foolish I was in failing to understand their situations, largely because I had never truly experienced those specific challenges; my perspective was still immature.

Interestingly, despite their different journeys, Shrey and Kitty became the best of confidants. Their ability to deeply connect with one another over their personal struggles highlighted to me the importance of truly understanding other person's POV rather than making assumptions based solely on our own limited views.

Mid 20s: My best friend in

...a mid-life crisis!

Lesson: To be patient while helping. Support system helps.
While visiting my childhood best friend aka *"chuddy buddy"* in Bangalore, we organized a dinner get-together with some close friends from our school days. Over the weekend, as I spent more time with him, it became clear that something was off. I noticed he was overwhelmed by constant overthinking and worrying about life and his future and he often resorted to excessive smoking in solitude. To give some background, he is one of the most intelligent people I know and it seemed that this very gift, his intelligence, was ironically contributing to his struggles. His mind was constantly racing trapping him in a cycle of over-analysis and negative thoughts. Although I couldn't fully grasp the depths of what he was experiencing or the specific thoughts occupying his mind, one thing was undeniably clear—he wasn't himself and looked off-color, a silent yet alarming sign of mental distress.
When I returned to my hometown, deeply concerned I attempted to discuss his situation with his parents. To my surprise, they dismissed my concerns. Their response was one I have often heard in traditional households—"Once he gets married, everything will fall into place". They were convinced that finding him a suitable girl and getting him married would magically solve everything.
I strongly opposed their viewpoint, arguing that this could put both him and his future spouse in a difficult and unfair situation. For those who don't know, in arranged marriages,

partners get to know each other only after the match is fixed and sometimes even after the wedding itself. I vehemently objected to expecting marriage to be a cure, all when he clearly needed help. Instead, I suggested seeking professional help from a psychologist, as I honestly had no clue how to navigate this situation. However, despite my efforts, his parents took no action. Instead, they intensified their search for a bride, unknowingly adding more pressure on my friend, who was in no state to handle such expectations.

I felt completely helpless. This was when I truly understood the significance of a strong support system—when a family fails to acknowledge or help during a crisis, the situation becomes even more dire.

Determined not to give up on my best friend, I took one month of remote work from the office and told him that I would stay with him for a while. However, upon my return, his subsequent behavior was marked by withdrawal as he barely spoke to me. As the days passed, I saw his depression reaching its peak. He confined himself to his room, not going to work, avoiding any outings and even ignoring home-cooked meals. Instead, he spent his days binge-watching Netflix, ordering his favorite junk food and taking frequent smoke breaks.

To an outside observer, he might have appeared to be living a carefree, indulgent life. But I knew the truth—he was drowning in his own thoughts and desperately needed help. I decided the first step was to convince him to stop drinking and smoking. When I brought it up, he was resistant, saying he wasn't ready to quit just yet. I didn't push him but instead calmly emphasized how these habits were only worsening his mental and physical health. He listened and after some reflection, he promised to give it a try when he felt ready and expressed a firm belief that if he truly set his mind to something, he could achieve it.

Here is something I have learned about addictions, in general —Firstly, no matter how little money you have, you will always find a way to afford them. Secondly, while external counseling and support can help, it ultimately comes down to the individual's self-belief to break free from harmful habits. A strong support system can be a guiding light, but the real change must come from within.

I somehow convinced him to join a community fitness club together. During that time, I was also occupied with too much work. We both faced our own struggles, but we remained consistent and disciplined. We committed to our daily routine, showing up at 5 a.m. every morning. On some days, he wouldn't work out at all—he would simply sit, nail-biting and lost in the cyclone of thoughts. But I kept engaging him in meaningful conversations and pep talks that gradually made him feel more at ease. Over time, the discipline started paying off.

One of the most significant benefits of engaging in regular physical exercise is that it naturally leads to the development of healthier habits. Gradually, you find yourself less inclined toward alcohol and smoking and build upon positive changes in your lifestyle—changes that can significantly cut off the *"water supply"* feeding the plant of depression. Eventually, he completely gave up smoking and drinking. The transformation was evident—not just physically, but mentally and emotionally as well.

At that point, I felt at peace, knowing that he had overcome this difficult phase. Both of us noticed a remarkable improvement in our overall fitness and it was then that I felt a profound sense of peace, knowing he had overcome such a major obstacle.

I was filled with gratitude and overwhelmed by the experience of being part of his transformative journey. It taught me invaluable life lessons about understanding others' struggles from their perspectives and more importantly about the patience and empathy required to truly support someone through tough times.

Late 20s: Work-Life balance

Lesson: A paycheck isn't worth you.

Across many Indian societies, there exists a persistent narrative that promotes the belief that our profession is larger than our life. A job should not encapsulate who you are or define your entire identity. To assert that what you do is the only reflection of your value is to diminish the rich complexity of being human. There is so much more to each person and we deserve the opportunity to flourish in ways that extend so much beyond our professional lives. Yes, it provides the means to put food on the table and yes, it can be a source of genuine passion. And when that passion is present, obstacles and limitations often seem to vanish, allowing you to pursue your work with unbridled enthusiasm. However, we must not let our jobs overshadow our broader existence. It should never be the sole measure of your self-worth.

I believe one of the most admirable qualities of today's Gen Z generation is their commitment to pursuing paths that truly fulfill them. I am inspired by so many young innovators around me hustling their own trails. My younger cousin sister launched an e-commerce startup and my juniors from my school started an AI-driven healthcare venture. I must acknowledge that today's youth has a confident professional mindset — of transformation, challenges and the ultimate decision to choose a more fulfilling life alongside the career. I have witnessed so many young individuals willingly forgo financially lucrative opportunities in favor of choices that resonate with their principles and values—something I doubt I would have dared to do when I was just starting out my career. Many of the millennials entered the field of engineering because it represented a safe, secure option and selected professions based on financial stability. However, this new generation exhibits the courage to choose paths that not only align with their principles and values but also provide them with genuine fulfillment. I find this approach brilliant, as it is exactly how true change-makers are born.

Ultimately, we all yearn to see a meaningful impact arising from our daily work; if the outcome is unclear, murky or a wishy-washy corporate answer, then we are simply choosing to steer clear of fulfillment and content in our work life. Acknowledging that the willingness to take risks is highest in our 20s—as future responsibilities might dampen that spirit—it is the best time to pursue our dreams.

Each one of us faces many unfamiliar challenges throughout our professional career, like adapting from a typical 9-to-5 job initially to being available 24/7 as I shouldered higher work responsibilities, balancing personal and professional life and coping with the unpredictability of the market forces. I addressed these challenges by implementing strict time management strategies, setting boundaries between work and personal time and developing a strong process-driven approach to ensure smooth operations and greater work-life balance.

Embracing a greater people management role, I quickly realized that real-world decisions are not solely based on spreadsheets; they blend in individual backgrounds, perspectives, egos, pride, marketing strategies and unique motivations. Initially, it was challenging for me to grasp and adapt to this complexity. However, I was also aware that my diverse upbringing and exposure to different work cultures provided me with a unique advantage. I overcame such challenges effectively by applying transferrable soft skills and people skills. I honed my ability to understand and appreciate different viewpoints and be humble which has enabled me to navigate complex interpersonal dynamics with empathy and insight. Overcoming these obstacles has been immensely rewarding, reinforcing my self-belief.

Looking back on my days, I'm amazed at how far I have come. The unconventional path we chose is not always easy, but it is incredibly rewarding—and opens up many opportunities for exploration. For example, this book is a result of such an effort. Life can be beautifully unpredictable and sometimes all it takes is the courage to take a chance and enjoy the ride.

Checkmate by life!

Lesson: Mental health issues can trigger even when you are doing great in life.

Some days we are on a high but that high soon plummets into one of the darkest times.

Michael Phelps, the greatest Olympian of all time, struggled with anxiety, depression and substance abuse throughout his celebrated career. Phelps dedicated his life to training for a race that lasted less than a minute—which determined whether he succeeded or failed. This amount of pressure is immense, enough to break even the toughest humans and he achieved greatness beyond anything anyone could have ever dreamt of. But still, he was in such a dark place that he considered ending his life. He knew that he was the strongest person but at that moment he realized he was the weakest.

Following his suspension from USA Swimming, Phelps recognized he could no longer ignore his mental health and needed help to overcome his situation. He was unsure how to open up and ask for help. But later realized that once he had asked for help everything became so easy and that decision saved his life. By opening up about his struggles, vulnerability and sharing the pain of hitting rock bottom transformed his outlook, he sparked an important conversation about mental health in sports.

He literally drew back the curtains on the topic which had a ripple effect in the world of professional sports, where admitting to mental health struggles has long been seen as a weakness. Athletes like gymnast Simone Biles, who stepped away from the Tokyo Olympics where she was touted to break the ceiling, tennis star Naomi Osaka at the

2021 French Open and cricketers Amelia Kerr and Glenn Maxwell took indefinite breaks over mental health. The current generation of top-level athletes tends to prioritize their well-being over competing at all costs. Their actions have shifted public perception and reduced the stigma associated with mental health challenges and I love the fact that people are showering their love and support.

There are no roses without thorns, no garden without weeds, no river without bends and no human without flaws. Still, there is a massive, common but flawed, notion that human beings are supposed to be born and live in an ideal way, always be kind and never show our darker side. In reality, this expectation forces us to hide our true selves. When we look at our base operating system closely, we have an inherent duality: one side harbors negative traits such as fear, selfishness and greed, while the other radiates empathy, honesty and kindness. We are always in a tussle due to these two energies which complement each other at different points in our life. Navigating the tension between these opposing forces is a fundamental, albeit ironic, part of being human.

We all experience ups and downs- a roller coaster ride especially in our 20s. So it is important to remember that you do not have to face these challenges alone. Asking for help is a sign of strength—not weakness. In fact, asking for help is one of the most courageous things you can do. And also you do not have to wait until you hit rock bottom to ask for help either.

While vulnerability is a scary word for a lot of people including me, to admit that you are struggling is the first step toward healing. Trust me, those small moments of opening up are initially discomforting but completely worth it in the end and could save your life.

CHAPTER THREE

Emotions

One of life's peculiar challenges is that you cannot trust your subjective sensation about how it is going while you are doing it. Of course, you will have feelings about the work but those feelings are constantly shifting with time; transient in nature. Actually, our current feelings often mislead us about our overall direction. Over the years, I have learnt that nearly all our strong feelings are fleeting. We are often widely delighted and deeply discouraged in the space of a single day. What feels overwhelmingly true at the moment may look entirely different in retrospect from a vantage point in the future.

A therapist once introduced me to a simple yet effective tool for gaining clarity. This framework allows you to step back and evaluate your choices by weighing potential gains and losses in all situations. For example, imagine you have moved to a big city like Delhi, leaving behind a cherished home filled with family, pets and lovely memories. Naturally, you might feel a strong pull to return. By applying this framework, you map out all these factors and the exercise reveals what you will gain from the move against what you might lose.

To help you assess your situation, draw a quadrant with four boxes as below:

- In the top right, label it "plus-plus"—this represents all the benefits of staying in Delhi.
- In the top left, write "plus-minus"—consider the positive outcomes you might lose if you don't stay.
- In the bottom left, mark it "minus-plus"—reflect on what you would miss if you remained.
- And in the bottom right, label it "minus-minus"—think about the negatives you'd avoid by leaving.

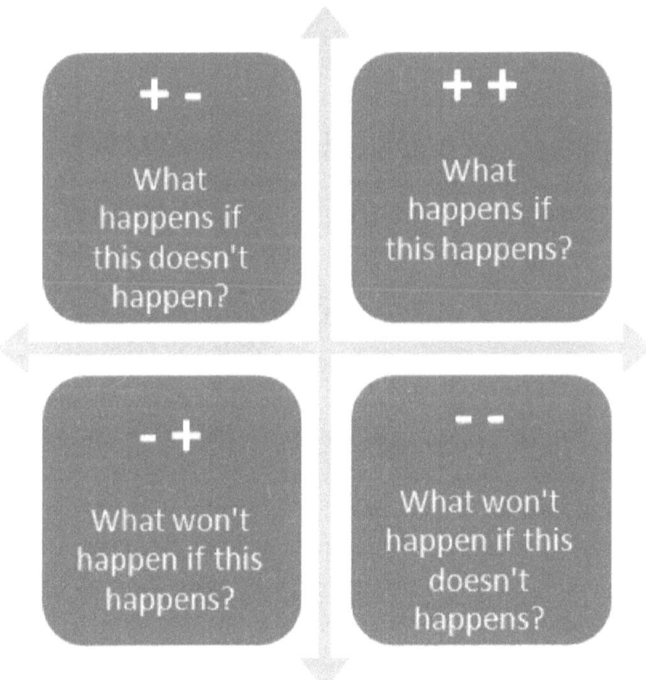

When emotions overwhelm you, pause, take a deep breath and use this simple tool. While it is perfectly natural to feel deeply, remember that you are not defined by your emotions. They ebb and flow like waves—we can acknowledge them without clinging to them, simply riding them out.

We generally manage our feelings in one of three ways: cherish, ignore or battle with them. I learned this lesson during one of the most soul-shattering experiences of my life. As someone who thrives on adventure—be it on land, in the air or underwater—I always believed I had mastered my fear. Jumping from high platforms and navigating risky terrains came naturally to me. However, one seemingly ordinary day at Bir Billing, a world-renowned paragliding spot, completely changed that belief.

I was enjoying breakfast at a café with a group of friends who were preparing to take flight. I had even shared an engaging conversation with a fellow adventurer Varun, who was also an experienced skydiver. I chewed his brain discussing advanced technology in his Garmin sports watch and our mutual passion for aerial sports. After finishing my meal, I settled into a quiet corner with my laptop to catch up on some work. An hour later, the atmosphere shifted abruptly when an instructor burst into the café, visibly distressed and clutching a first aid kit. I enquired what happened and I learned that Varun had been in a serious accident.

Without hesitation, I abandoned my work and followed him. Minutes later, we arrived at the scene to find the lifeless body of a young pilot—Varun, whose glider had collapsed midair after a spiral fall. Unsure of what to do next, the instructor and I carefully lifted his body and placed it in a car. Our first stop was a nearby hospital, only to discover there was neither a doctor nor an ambulance available. We then embarked on a two-hour journey to the next facility, during which Varun lay motionless with his head resting on my lap. Barely a word was exchanged during the drive. The silence was heavy with shock and grief until we reached the hospital where the doctors declared him dead and kept his body in the mortuary.

After returning back in the night, I took a long, hot shower and tried to process and soak in the day's events. For the first time in my life, I was gripped by a paralyzing fear. I surrendered to the situation. I resigned myself to being powerless and stuck. I spent the entire night trembling and crying. The following day, returning to the café felt surreal. The once vibrant space was now filled with sorrow—familiar faces marked by grief. I learned that Varun, who had recently married, had come to Bir Billing seeking solace after a personal conflict with his wife. At that moment, I felt an overwhelming urge to leave and retreat to the comfort of my family, yet something within me urged me to stay. I made a tough decision not to run away like a coward, and instead stay to support my close-knit flying community and face my emotions directly.

The next few days were marked by raw vulnerability as we all shared our pain. Although the experienced flyers gradually returned to the skies, every time I saw a paraglider, I was haunted by the image of Varun's still form. I confronted that fear day after day, and finally, after a week, I managed to fly again—even if only briefly. In that fleeting moment aloft, I sensed that even the deepest scars can begin to mend when courage takes flight.

This harrowing incident left an indelible mark on my character and worldview. I decided that I wanted to serve and rescue others, that I would volunteer to boost morale, would give talks to spread awareness. I didn't care how menial the tasks would be I would be there. A sense of purpose surrounded me and I came to this realization to serve society in a positive way. The timing was uncanny though. It led me to specialize in First Responders and Search and Rescue. Now I actively lead and help authorities in Search and Rescue operations and provide First Aid in disaster-prone and resource-constricted high-altitude Himalayan regions. I successfully turned my fear into a life motto of saving human lives by looking straight into its eyes. I no longer perceive these exhilarating pursuits as mere adventures; they have transformed into a deep commitment to save and inspire others to save lives. The honor I get on these missions does not equate to an entire career.

CHAPTER FOUR

Support system

I cannot underline more how a robust support network is essential in the journey of life. Sharing your thoughts with a few trusted individuals in your corner—be it a caring family, close friends or a significant other—can truly be the game changer in tough situations. Support of loved ones encourages you to keep moving forward. The support system comes in handy at times when you are not feeling your best. Having a supportive partner is essential—if not parents' support, as it can truly prove make or break determine your success. Also, therapists, doctors and other health professionals can step in and provide professional support if and when needed.

And if you have time-tested friends, count yourself lucky in life. I recall a friend who lives by an amazing rule in their friend circle, a simple yet powerful rule: **"No crying alone".** If you're overwhelmed and sense that tears are inevitable, pick up the phone and reach out—because sharing your sorrow can make all the difference. To me, this willingness to sit with someone in their darkest moments encapsulates the essence of being human.

This idea extends to a very important conversation. When our friends are struggling our instinct is to rescue them, pull them out of the mud and fix them instantly. Even if it is well-intentioned, unsolicited advice or premature fixes usually feel more invasive than supportive. Sometimes it is just a horrible feeling from the victim's perspective. Because more often than not what looks like the natural next step in one's life might be the hardest step to take on from their POV. In such situations, the lesser said is much better than more being said outside of that.

True friendship is not about extracting someone from their challenges, but it is your willingness to sit in the mud with them until they are ready to say let's get out now. There is a unique healing power in simply being present through someone's difficult times. Believe me, it is so healing and cathartic that makes your life something greater than yourself when you help another person.

This concept is also reflected in the globally well-known 12-step programs for overcoming substance or behavioral addictions. In that, the final step is the most critical and if you can master the final 12th step you are more likely to win the battle in hand. The final step—**"Service"**—is about helping others, emphasizing that those who have supported someone through hardship often learn the most about themselves and life.

In my 20s I have learned that the quality of our relationships will have a direct and profound influence on the ability to push beyond our own limits. Just one person who believes in you—who says, "You got this, and I am here for you no matter what the results are"—can unlock reserves of courage and energy you never knew existed.

We often fail to realize that deeply fulfilling relationships are the unseen backbone of a happy and successful life. Also, we falsely think that we have to face challenges and responsibilities all alone, but instead sharing them with a community or a close friend can make all the difference, preventing burnout. Because as an individual we do not have the energy but in a relationship, friendship or community it is remarkable.

Goodwill of strangers as a Support

In the tapestry of life, the kindness of strangers often emerges as an unexpected yet supportive thread. A simple act of goodwill—a warm smile, a compassionate word, a helping hand—can illuminate our lives. These gestures, seemingly small, carry the power to uplift our spirits and remind us of our shared humanity. The beauty of this unconditional support lies in its spontaneity and purity. Unlike the bonds formed by long-standing relationships, the kindness of a stranger is free of expectations or obligations.

I recall a beautiful incident that unfolded during the third wave of COVID-19—a moment that affirmed the unexpected power of strangers' goodwill. I was solo traveling for 3 months in South India at that time. After exploring the enchanting Wayanad, I set my sights on Coorg, famously known as the "Scotland of India" due to its landscape and climate reminiscent of Scotland. To reach Coorg, I had to cross from Kerala into Karnataka through the dense jungles of Bandipore National Park. Given that Kerala was a notorious hotspot for COVID cases, state border crossings required a valid RT-PCR report taken within the past 48 hours. I opted for public transport, hoping to bypass this requirement, but fate had another plan. The bus I boarded refused to cross the border—it dropped me just 100 meters before the state border and then made a U-turn, leaving me the sole passenger continuing on foot in a jungle area with no apparent means of transportation.

I saw on the Karnataka side, a temporary medical booth was set up. Three nurses—famously referred to as "sisters" in India—sat in their crisp white sari attire, with a register to record details of passersby. As I walked with my trolley bag (back then, I used to backpack with a trolley bag—an amusing quirk of my travels), I paid little attention to their calls. However, their repeated and resounding call of "RT-PCR" could have easily reached a semi-deaf person. Finally, I looked up as they beckoned me with raised hands. I presented them with my most recent RT-PCR report, which was over a week old and thus invalid as per the norms. By this time, it became clear that the sisters communicated in only Kannada or Malayalam—languages I did not understand at all—rather than in English or Hindi. They hand signaled me to return to the Kerala side, but that was not a viable option. I had already taken the last bus, and the nearest RT-PCR testing center was a six-hour journey away. Even if I managed to get tested, the procedure would have taken place the next day, with the report arriving a day or two later—plus another six-hour ride back. My calculations revealed that I would be losing at least four days; therefore, going back was simply not an option.

Desperate, I requested that they allow me to proceed, reasoning that I had spent the entire past week in the jungle with minimal human contact. I even suggested that they could conduct a rapid test or check my body temperature for an immediate assessment. Yet, my pleas were met with indifference and they instead mockingly told me to return to the jungle. When my further attempts to convince them faltered, they signaled toward a policeman in charge for additional authority. This policeman was a giant bald man with a stern demeanor and a prominent mustache, stationed at a police chowki diagonally across the road. He was more reminiscent of a villain from a South Indian movie than a police officer. I approached him hesitantly, keeping a respectful distance of a few steps and requested his assistance as politely as possible. Although he understood a bit more English than the sisters, he too dismissed my requests.

In India, such situations with police are often resolved by invoking the phrase *"chacha vidhayak hai hamare"*—implying a certain political clout. I tried to leverage this informal influence, but it also went in vain. After 20 minutes of intense but unfruitful negotiation, I resolutely sat down on the footpath a few meters away from the nurses' camp. They assumed that my silence meant I would eventually leave, yet I was determined to stay. I observed that a couple of cars managed to cross the border—their passengers' RT-PCR reports being checked and noted in registers—while I seemed to have no escape.

After an hour of waiting on that footpath, my eyes lit up when an ice cream vendor appeared seemingly out of nowhere on his cycle. I was certain that this poor guy would not be able to show any report. As he passed the booth, he was stopped and signaled three by one sister to offer three ice-creams before riding off. One of the sisters was not in the mood for an ice cream. The sisters then offered the ice creams to the policeman, who also declined them and instead suggested that they be given to me. The sisters looked at me and extended the offer. I nodded in agreement with a cute puppy-like expression. We exchanged a very warm, genuine smile and they beckoned me over. I quickly returned to my spot on the footpath and began feasting on the ice cream, feeling relief after more than an hour of tense waiting. All three of them shared giggles as they saw me enjoy my treat. To my amazement, even the stern policeman smiled. He approached me and advised that I cross the border quickly after finishing my ice cream, as darkness was fast approaching.

I savored what turned out to be the best ice cream of my life. Lifting my trolley bag, I expressed heartfelt gratitude to everyone as I passed by, leaving behind an atmosphere filled with smiles and warmth.

That day, I learned three very important lessons:

1. When requests and pressure fall short, a shared moment of smile/laughter can work wonders.
2. Language is only one aspect of communication—we can connect with others on a much deeper level even without it.
3. The goodwill of strangers can manifest in the most unexpected ways.

In a world that can sometimes feel isolating, these moments of shared humanity serve as gentle beacons where we witness the true essence of community—guiding us back to the comforting realization that we are all walking this journey together.

CHAPTER FIVE

Relationships

One of the most talked about things in the 20s is adult relationships. This is a time when many of us search for a loving partner, even as we juggle careers and studies. Navigating adult relationships can feel both exhilarating and bewildering and that has always intrigued us. Whether it's a fling, orbiting, benching, casual dating, live-in, marriage, situationship, nanoship etc, the array of Gen Z dating terms can be overwhelming. And often, it's hard to pin down exactly what kind of relationship we are in.

A few years ago I attended the beautiful destination wedding of a colleague and a dear friend in Udaipur. After nearly five years of dating, his marriage was essentially a perfect blend of college love and an arranged setup. After the *phera* concluded around 2 a.m., while we were casually chilling, the conversation unexpectedly turned to relationships and marriage. Our group which was attending the wedding consisted of ten young people all in their late 20s—two bachelors and eight married individuals. Interestingly, only three of the married couples appeared to be truly happy, while the remaining five seemed to be struggling, their marriages barely holding on by a thread. There is a traditional rasam where, upon the groom's arrival on horseback, it is believed that the first person to step onto the horse will be the first to marry. Previously, there used to be very fierce competition among the bachelors for that coveted spot. However, this time, all the bachelors were noticeably reluctant, with not a single one even attempting it—a reflection of the general apprehension towards marriage among young adults today.

Due to work commitments, he had to move to Europe for sometime. Only a month after the wedding, I received a distressed call from him. His voice was seemingly laced with worry and sadness. I tried to lift his spirits by asking about his honeymoon phase and how things were progressing, but my light-hearted questions did little to ease his overwhelming anxiety and emotional turmoil. Gradually, as I calmed him down, he began to open up and share the reasons behind his distress—all of which were connected to his married life. I took a deep breath and absorbed every word, carefully restraining myself from jumping in with advice because I knew that probably would not help. After all, marriage is a big thing not just for the couple, but for their families as well. Instead, I simply encouraged him to remain positive and allow time for the situation to settle.

A few days later, the same cycle repeated—and then again a few days after that. By this point, he had begun drinking and smoking excessively out of anxiety. The situation escalated when, after a major fight the previous day, his wife blocked him. Despite this, he refused to give up, reaching out persistently by emailing and calling from different numbers, desperate to resolve the conflict immediately rather than letting it fester. And the circumstances of being distant and in different time zones added to the woes. I began to recognize a familiar pattern in his stories: he was pushing hard for love, while his partner needed space to settle down and nurture her own feelings.

Love is an emotion—something deeply personal and experienced uniquely by each individual. We each define and seek it in our own way. There is no absolute right or wrong here, but it became evident that their love was not blossoming because he was not being true to himself. Often, people in such situations end up sinking those they are closest to further into despair.

Out of insecurity, we sometimes try to control our partner, which inadvertently only builds tension. We need to understand the very facet of love that it is a flow of freedom. When you allow someone the freedom to be themselves, they flourish—and that authentic energy deepens the connection. Conversely, restricting that freedom may lead to pretended affection and mounting insecurity.

Though I consider myself non-judgmental, I could clearly sense from his narratives that he was unknowingly on the wrong path and I gently conveyed this to him. I took it upon myself to help extricate himself from the emotional quagmire in which he was mired. He loves travelling so I suggested he take a small break and witness the magical Northern Lights in Finland. I knew he also loved working out at the gym, yet he had not been doing so for over a month since his marriage. I urged him to set aside all the negative stuff and return to the gym. He quickly reasoned that he could not commit to a routine as of now due to his current travel schedule. I reassured him, suggesting that even attending the gym a few days a week would be beneficial. I emphasized that his primary focus should be on engaging in activities he genuinely loved, rather than overthinking every aspect of his current turmoil.

I assured him that not only would this help him reconnect with himself, but it would also grant his wife the much-needed space. And in the worst case even if nothing else improved, at least he would be in good health and mental space to deal with things. Although he was convinced, he remained somewhat reluctant to stop obsessing over the situation. Yet, deep down, I was confident that embarking on this journey of self-discovery and doing something he was truly passionate about would eventually bring him the balance he needed.

A few weeks later, he returned to India. He sounded genuinely happy and positive. His very first words were, "You were right, brother". He shared that he had resumed a regular gym routine, had quit smoking and drinking and that his marriage had taken a positive turn. They were even planning a vacation shortly and we discussed some exciting destinations for it. For the first time since his marriage, our entire conversation was filled with positive energy—a change that brought immense relief to both of us and we genuinely felt it that day!

The significance of this story lies in its call to return to simplicity—highlighting the truth that love is inherently simple yet profound. By imposing complex expectations and definitions, the natural flow of emotions gets hindered. However, at its core, love is an uncomplicated experience which is sought to be embraced in its most genuine form.

I have observed that we tend to overcomplicate the seemingly simple nature of love. Embracing the below insights can help us approach relationships with clarity and balance, transforming complexity into an opportunity for love and meaningful connections.

1. ***Recognize the Subtle Green Flags***: We often overlook the small, positive signs—those green flags—that signal a healthy relationship. Ironically, while these cues are plentiful, most of the singles lament their scarcity. By overlooking them and placing too much emphasis on the *"vibe match"*, we set ourselves up in an unfavorable position right from the beginning. Initially, everyone is inclined to present themselves as the best option available out there. The more time we spend together, the more layers are gradually stripped away, ultimately revealing our true nature. While it is often said that time is a great healer, I would add that it is also a great peeler.

2. ***Embrace Space for Personal Growth:*** One common pitfall is neglecting the need for personal space. Even simple practices, like spending quiet time together without words, can open the door to a more genuine, energy-filled bond. You will feel uncomfortable initially but then you expose yourself as a human being and slowly start to feel the person's energy on a different level.

3. ***Cultivate Patience:*** Our generation is known for being fast-paced, but building a solid and beautiful relationship demands a lot of patience and perseverance. Genuine connections do not develop overnight; the most rewarding relationships are the ones that take time to mature.

4. ***Start with Self-Happiness:*** Finally, never burden someone else with the sole responsibility of making you happy. Establishing a strong relationship with yourself is essential before inviting someone else into your life. Too often, the fear of being alone drives us into relationships that fill an emotional void—but these are rarely sustainable. True contentment starts from within and only then can you truly share happiness with others.

5. ***Four pillars of relationships***: Great relationships, in my view, adhere to what I call the *"four table leg rule"*. This rule is built on the pillars of intellectual compatibility, emotional compatibility, physical compatibility and the circumstances of life. These components are not constant; they rise and fall like waves, so when one aspect weakens, the others must be strong enough to support the relationship as a whole. While it is possible to sustain a good relationship with only two or three of these elements, achieving a great one requires all four.

CHAPTER SIX

Friendships

It is often said that you are the average of the five people you spend the most time with and the derivative saying, *"Show me your friends and I will show you your future"* carries the very same meaning. Regardless of which version you have encountered, the underlying intent remains unchanged.

Is it possible to reflect on your life without mentioning the significance of friends? Overlooking them would undoubtedly be a major oversight and blunder, wouldn't it? In the tender passage of our 20s, friendship becomes both a mirror and a mosaic. This decade is a canvas splashed with vibrant hues of ambition, uncertainty and discovery and the friends we make along the way add strokes of color that define our journey. As we forge our identities and navigate new experiences, these bonds offer more than companionship. They provide a safe space to share our dreams, vulnerabilities and countless moments of joy and heartache.

As previously discussed, a solid support system is an integral part of your life. While the backing of family is great to have, there is absolutely no one who can replicate the unique role that friends play in our lives. I consider myself fortunate to have a wealth of friends by my side.

And I take great pride in admitting that as I enter my 30s, I still have frequent contact with many from my kindergarten days.

These enduring connections fill me with both nostalgia and gratitude—memories of shared laughter over midnight cups of coffee, every spontaneous adventure and even the quiet moments of understanding (at least trying to be). Every now and then, we find ourselves exchanging simple pleasures of pulling each other's legs or reminiscing about *"the good old days"*. Whether we are wrestling with the uncertainties of a budding career or coping with the pains of heartbreak, there is a silent acknowledgment of our friends' unwavering support, no matter the distance or the ever-changing situations in our lives. Similarly, a friend's quiet humor and steadfast presence can transform even the bleakest day into a remarkable adventure. Each story, told with both laughter and a touch of wistfulness, stitch together the tapestry of our lives. We speak of dreams that have evolved over time, of challenges that have tested our resolve and of secrets that feel like a precious treasure. Our conversations meander like a familiar, cherished song—one that has played through years of joy and struggle alike.

Whenever I reunite with my old friends, I see their eyes radiate the warmth of countless shared memories. In those rooftop cafés, bathed in the golden glow of an autumn sun, I realized that the true beauty of life resides not in fleeting moments, but in the timeless bonds that have carried us through every twist and turn. In a world that is ever-changing, these enduring friendships serve as a reminder that time, no matter how relentless in its march forward, only deepens the roots of genuine connection.

A heartfelt shout-out to the friends who stay up late to talk to you through things, respond immediately when problems arise, drop everything to help and basically be a therapist. They don't get enough credit but they are the jewels in our life.

In my early twenties, I was surrounded by so many cool friends that even after dividing into two cricket teams, there were still enough people to take on the roles of match referees. Yet, gradually and inevitably, they began to vanish. Someone's job was stressful, someone's marriage demanded too much, someone's parents became unwell, someone had children at an early age and another's time zone shifted. I moved on to playing badminton when four of them remained, then to tennis when only two left and now I find myself considering running a marathon alone next year. Just kidding.

I honestly believe that we are also the reason for it. We always place immense value on and endlessly romanticize love and relationships, often at the expense of our friendships. We tend to take friendships for granted and friendship, in turn, happily accepts that treatment. We give so many dating entrance exams to clear for one elusive love, but friendship is always a mass bunk right from the start. We give so many auditions for love, performing regularly with high efforts and sacrifices like even altering who we were in the process. We learn new languages for love, yet in our friendships, a few emoticons are deemed enough. Love demands responsibility, but friendship is bonded over a shared sense of irresponsibility. For years, I proudly boasted about how my brother was such an incredible friend, that no matter how much time passed, we always picked up right where we left off. But, over time, we all simply...fell away.

The very strength of friendship is also its inherent weakness: everything is forgiven, accepted and allowed. There is so much understanding in our friendships, that when it ends we even understand that also.

CHAPTER SEVEN

Travel

"Jobs fill your pocket, travel fills your soul."

Travel began to follow an entirely different course in my life. My very first solo journey took place when I was 24—way longer than it should have been. My progress was gradual as I moved forward steadily. Driven by a deep passion for understanding diverse cultures, I have extensively traveled and explored over 15+ countries and 25+ states within India as I turned 30.

I found the experience of travelling to be unusually rewarding. Through travel, I embraced new experiences, cultures and perspectives. Each journey concluded with a profound sense of relief and elation, as though I had been liberated from a weight I had not even realized I was carrying. Whenever I visit remote corners of the world, I often feel a renewed perspective of who I truly am. Over time, travel evolved into something more explicit and deeply personal than I had ever imagined it would become, leaving me both invigorated and emboldened to embark on even more challenging quests of self-discovery.

During my first international trip, I encountered an unexpected setback when my laptop bag was stolen upon my arrival in Rome. The bag contained two of my laptops and my wallet—which held all my cards and cash. I was left with my passport in hand and a trolley bag of clothes. I was stranded only to find shelter with a lovely Romanian family of my cab driver. They graciously hosted me for several days, providing me with shelter and support while I managed to procure new cards and secure other essential items. To help lift my spirits during this challenging time, they even arranged tickets for me to attend a Champions League football match. I remain close to them to this day.

Witnessing the great migration live in Kenya's Masai Mara National Park transformed the very chemistry of life's fundamentals. In Vietnam, I met a single mother full of grit and spirit overcoming hardships and conducting tours to support her twin daughters. We bonded over our love for exploring wartime history and local egg coffee. Navigating life with an explorer's heart has taught me so much about life and humanity—the power of hope, resilience and the transformative potential of business. I gained a tremendous amount of wisdom through my travels. It was an amazing means to develop several key people and soft skills as below:

- *Adaptability:* Venturing beyond my comfort zone and adjusting to new cultures has empowered me to thrive in dynamic environments.
- *Creativity:* Observing how people in various countries approach challenges has inspired me to bring more creative ideas to my life.
- *Diversity:* Collaborating alongside individuals from different cultural backgrounds has enriched my perspective, giving me a truly diverse outlook on life.

- *Networking:* Building my network from scratch has enhanced my ability to forge and nurture meaningful connections.

Traveling does NOT have to be expensive. Rather than assuming that you must emulate modern travel influencers who showcase extravagant floating breakfasts or bathtubs adorned with rose petals, understand that such displays are the very antithesis of genuine travel. It is not about spending money or chasing luxury—it's about immersing yourself in real experiences and uncovering the answers that only the journey itself can provide.

I encourage you, at least once, to say yes to solo travel. Let it surprise you, intimidate you, make you feel lonely, joyful, overwhelmed, angry and every conceivable emotion that possibly exists. Witness firsthand how much you are capable of accomplishing on your own. Where you are independent, where no one is your friend and everyone is your friend. You build deeper connections with different people—spending late nights in conversation with your hostel roommates—while also facing the discomfort of solitary meals, engaging in introspective conversations with yourself and uncovering aspects of yourself you never knew existed. Dare to experiment with the version of yourself you have always wanted to become, but were held back in the fear of judgment. Embrace the vast, overwhelming spectrum of life and fully immerse yourself in every experience it presents – all the good and all the bad. Let that experience find you, just one time. After that journey, you can decide whether to continue traveling alone or that it isn't meant for you. But please, don't make that decision without ever having tried it. Trust me. ♥

Apni vyast zindagi se thoda time nikal lena kyunki na promotion yaad rhega, na projects, na deadlines. Bas yaad rhega to ye safar aur kuch kahanaiyaan...

So where should we travel?

Perhaps, we are not meant to know. Let the road decide where to go. That is actually the essence of travelling. Those who have traveled far and wide will understand that travel has never been solely about reaching a destination—it has always been about the journey. Life has taught me not to take plans and itineraries too seriously. There is already a greater plan designed for us. Our task is simply to recognize and follow the subtle signs and gentle nudges that continuously guide us forward.

So, have you ever embarked on a solo journey?

If you have, please feel free to DM me and share your crazy experiences. And if you haven't yet taken that leap, I would be delighted to hear your opinions, fears or any obstacles that might be holding you back.

A fun fact about me is that whenever I travel, I never post any pictures or updates on social media. I believe I am traveling solely for the pure joy of the experience, without the need for external validation.

CHAPTER EIGHT

20 life lessons of my 20s

Knowing "*Who I am Not*" is the first step of knowing "*Who am I*". As I enter my 30's, I may not yet have a definitive vision of what I want in life, but I am certainly clearer about what I don't want in life. I will share the 20 hard learned life lessons of my 20s. It took me a long time to realize, simple things in life.

That relationships require understanding and patience.

That love can fade away.

That people betray you even if they once promised otherwise.

That self-care is extremely important.

That Health and happiness come first no matter what.

That it's alright to take breaks and prioritize mental health.

To go on solo trips and solo dates.

To want different things at different stages of your life as we keep evolving.

It's not important to be answerable to everybody.

That to live happily you don't need to (and should not) depend on anybody.

(1) Live life to the fullest

"Life is not short, people start living late only. As long as the paths are understood, by then it is time to return."

Remembering famous Bollywood actor Late Irrfan Si whose words beautifully capture the notion that life isn't inherently short—it's simply that we often delay the moment when we begin to truly live.

20s is a period of boundless energy and potential. In this season of life, living to the fullest means embracing change, seizing opportunities and daring to dream beyond the horizon. This is the decade to step outside your comfort zone—whether that means traveling/hiking to far-off lands, diving into a new passion or simply exploring the depths of your own inner world. Each experience, whether triumphant or challenging, is a brushstroke on the masterpiece of your vibrant canvas. The thrill of the unknown fuels personal growth, teaching you lessons that no classroom ever could. They invite you to live passionately, love freely and embrace every twist and turn with open arms. When you look back, believe me, it won't be the moments of hesitation that you remember, but the adventures that made your heart soar.

(2) Self-growth

Your 20s are a precious time of discovery, self-growth and endless opportunities. One of the best ways to live this decade is by pampering yourself, not just with material gifts, but with experiences that will last a lifetime. Travel the world—immerse yourself in new cultures, meet new people, absorb different perspectives and experiment with your understanding of life. The journey is way more than just about seeing new places; it's about expanding your mind and broadening your understanding of the world. And if you do this, you might just find yourself in the process which is actually returning to your true self, before the world get its hand on you. The way you can understand yourself and self-reflect no one else can.

For self-growth, emotional intelligence is highly underrated yet it is perhaps the most critical skill. There is nothing soft about soft skills—especially EQ. It shapes your personal relationships, your professional success and your ability to lead with empathy. It empowers you to connect and build trust with others on a deeper level. Learning to understand the perspectives of others is an essential part of self-growth. Without it, we risk miscommunication, conflict and misunderstandings. Develop it ASAP before it hurts you in the long run and always, always make an effort to show kindness. Good deeds often have a ripple effect. You never know when your kindness will come back to you in unexpected ways.

(3) Don't fear to evolve perspectives

Over time, we become so deeply ingrained in life's philosophy that our ability to tweak, nudge, or transform ourselves gradually diminishes. I believe that if people are allowed to change their minds more frequently without fear of judgment, it could significantly accelerate human evolution. For example, if I held a strong belief five years ago and then drastically shifted my perspective today, society might hastily label that change as hypocrisy. In reality, however, such a transformation should be recognized as evolution. Shouldn't we all be more open and welcoming when people alter their viewpoints and adjust their societal positions on various matters over time?

We need to judge ourselves for our own happiness and what matters to us and not what society deems as successful. That is freedom in a true democratic sense of picking what someone wants will be allowed. That inculcation will only happen in a society that is not conformist which is not today but in a very utopian scenario if I had to paint it I would paint a world that would be like that.

(4) Learn new activities

In our twenties, the world stretches out like an uncharted map, full of promise and hidden treasures. Embracing a new activity during this transformative decade is not merely about acquiring a skill—it is also about daring to step beyond the familiar and into the realm of possibilities. Whether it's learning to play a musical instrument, picking up a new sport or exploring new businesses or creative arts, each endeavor invites us to rediscover our strengths, challenge our limits and evolve into richer versions of ourselves. In the process, we learn to appreciate not just the outcome, but the beautiful, evolving journey of personal growth. Keep learning continuously, as more often than not, there is always *"one more thing"* to discover.

(5) Starting is the most difficult part. Being disciplined is the next difficult part.

I will be the first one to tell you there were many days when I did not want to get out of bed —if I asked whether you wake up excited every day and if replied *"yes"*, I am going to blatantly call you a liar because we all know that this is far from the truth. However, if you have those small things or goals that get you excited on those reluctant days, it is definitely going to make it look better and easier for you at the end when you are getting ready for a presentation or whatever important task you are leading up to. Consider the greats in any walk of life: they push forward and do things even on days when motivation is scarce. And that is the separation, the difference is their mindset and unwavering discipline that sets them apart.

No matter the challenge, no matter how dark things get, there is always hope and you can emerge stronger on the other side. But we need to acknowledge that the real change does not happen overnight. It requires showing up every day and investing effort into your happiness and success even when it is hard. I would call it putting money into the bank so that at the end of the year or when the time comes we could withdraw that money that we had saved throughout the year.

(6) Obsessed with results

The key to a happy life is to accept that you are never in control, that way you are always more focused on the process in the present than the results in the future. The obsession with the outcome is actually a trap. When you are obsessed with the outcome you lose sight of the present. Instead, allow the outcome to unfold naturally. The amount of depression in our society these days is a consequence of how much we are crazy and preoccupied with these outcomes.

I have always viewed job interviews as one of the highest-pressure situations in my life. Reflecting on them, the ones in which I succeeded were often those where I showed up unprepared. Recently, I attended an interview that I intended to treat merely as a mock run for more critical opportunities ahead. In a surprising twist, I misread the timing 1-hour late in my head—thankfully, I had not misread the venue. It was a blunder that still leaves me in disbelief at how it happened. I acknowledged the error honestly and the panelists even complimented me on my apparent disregard for small details. It turned out to be a rather lovely way to kick off the interview process :p. Yet, these unexpected incidents occur in life without any forewarning I did not let it sway my mind and focused on what lay ahead. In the end, I literally nailed the interview and it turned out to be one of the best I could ever think of.

Most of the time, the answer is right there in front of us. Yet, our emotions and inner psyche possess such a strong influence that they cause us to become so narrowly fixated. We become so entrenched in believing that one notion is the only correct one that we choose to sideline the obvious.

(7) Whenever things are not going well, look inwards and focus on how you can improve and get better of the situation, rather than blaming others or external circumstances.

Often, we shy away from acknowledging our own shortcomings. The simple reason is first we need to be honest with ourselves and also muster a lot of strength and courage to accept that we are not perfect. Yet, recognizing that there are some shortcomings is the essential first step toward self-growth.

When you face any form of human competence, make every effort to first set your ego aside and learn. Learn to explore your weak areas, where you have a sense of insecurity. Allow yourself to be open and vulnerable, recognizing that genuine strength should not be mistaken for rigidity. As for me, every day I try to be a little more kinder, a little more compassionate and a little more aware not only of my inner self but of others around me. This is my therapy.

If you are willing to accept it, then you are open to self-reflection. You can always look to improve and reach out to people and ask for help and believe me there will be enough people to guide and support—be it your family or close friends whoever those may be. Remember, personal development is a continuous journey, and we're all a work in progress.

(8) Honesty is the best policy

Honesty, in my view, stands as one of life's most crucial virtues or ingredients. Yes, hard work, dedication and passion are also vital but unless you are honest to yourself, you cannot be honest and thereby genuinely connect with others.

It is not just about truth-telling—it's a multifaceted quality that underpins trust, accountability and growth. It enriches relationships, nurtures personal growth and supports a healthy, ethical community. Its impact influences every aspect of life from sound decision-making to emotional well-being. For adults navigating complex personal and professional landscapes with honesty can lead to deeper connections, improved decision-making and a more fulfilled, authentic life.

I have discovered that embracing honesty—both inwardly and outwardly—has consistently helped me navigate life's challenges and keep moving forward, especially through tough times.

(9) Never try to control the variables.

One thing I realized in my 20s is that the obsession with the results puts pressure on us. We often find ourselves trapped by thoughts like, *"What if this doesn't work out?"* or *"What if I don't win or get selected?"* When we are obsessed with the outcome we lose sight of the present. Instead, if we take care of whatever the controllables are, we can achieve the desired result and even if we don't get the desired result, we'll improve, adjust our approach and execute better when we get a chance to prove ourselves again. Life is like an infinite game; a journey with no end results or destination. It always tends to give a second chance to one who is brave enough and willing to play bold.

While it's good to have goals and human nature to worry about the future, what truly matters is controlling our instincts and focusing on the present. Take care of small steps: what needs to be done, what extra can be done, and soon those steps align to help us achieve our goals. Every small action counts. By focusing on constants rather than uncontrollable variables, we can influence the future through what we do in the here and now.

"*Worry is like a pyre, while thinking is like a cool rain. Do not worry, think instead.*"

There is wisdom in the saying, which means that worrying won't deliver results, but thoughtful reflection will. While it's good to have goals and human nature to worry about the future, what truly matters is controlling our instincts and focusing on the present and the constants rather than variables that are not in our hands. Take care of small steps:

what needs to be done, what extra can be done etc. These incremental efforts not only build a strong foundation and contribute a lot to achieving our goals but also ensure that even if we miss a target, we are better equipped to adjust our plans and succeed in the long run. What you are doing in the present will have an impact on the future.

(10) Don't be afraid to fall

"Does life ever pan out the way you want it to be? "

Life is like a circus filled with countless challenges, where failure is an inevitable companion (like Thanos :p). There will be moments of pain and discouragement that test you to your very core. However, if you want to change the world do not be afraid of these circuses. Instead, allow them to propel you forward, transforming each failure into a stepping stone towards self-growth and success.

Instead of allowing *fear of failure* to discourage us, we ought to view every setback as a valuable opportunity for learning.We all know that failure hurts, especially when it occurs repeatedly; yet, in hindsight, we don't acknowledge that failure carries a quiet, transformative power. Even if you fall flat on your face, at least you are falling forward. By embracing our shortcomings and learning to triumph over failures, we equip ourselves with an unstoppable resilience in every facet of our lives.

(11) Setbacks are a part of life

Zindagi ki yehi reet hai, haar ke baad hi jeet hai which means *This is the way of life: There's victory only after defeat.*

Each and every individual feels frustration, disappointment and anger when things are not going our way. Yet, none of these emotions are constructive. *"What needs to be done now?"* is more important than any of these emotions. By shifting our focus to immediate action, we can manage our emotions in a much better way. It's a very delicate thing to do. Even in your worst times if you are committed to walking the hard yards. That to me is the real test in life because that is eventually god's test. And if you are not up to the test then basically you are not being grateful and loyal to the opportunity that is out there. That is how I look at it.

It is absolutely human to feel negative emotions, and we all experience them at some point or the other. But I always try to maintain control over them and if I am able to do that then naturally my thinking will be more constructive. It allows me to concentrate on the process rather than just the outcome. I've found that the better I manage my emotions, my thinking becomes more and more productive and solution-oriented. If you are strong enough to give everything you have and still fail, you will be strong enough to let it all go. Strong enough to pick up all your pieces and start over.

I have adopted a thumb rule for it. I consider most of the time to be a good time either you are learning or you're enjoying what you have learned. Sometimes you win, and sometimes you lose; when you win, celebrate, and when you lose, learn. Either way, you are having a good time.

(12) Importance of breaks

If you find yourself in tough waters, one of the first steps is to break free from the cycle. This can be achieved through any activity, which will vary depending on the individual's personality and interests. People use different coping strategies to deal with stressful or challenging situations. Common ones include meditation, breathing exercises, spending time in nature, listening to music, taking a few minutes of solitude, talking to a trusted friend or therapist, simply taking a short break to recharge and engaging in hobbies or activities that bring them joy. It might take some trial and error to find out the coping strategies that work best for you.

We live in an incredibly fast-paced world and often at times get swayed away in the process of achieving our goals or milestones. This pace is completely antithetical or at odds with our emotional and psychological well-being. As a result, we can unknowingly overextend and overconsume ourselves and lose touch with who we are in the process. And the worst part is that we may not even realize it.

That's why it is so essential to take a breather amid the chaos. I have a personal rule that has served me well in managing this and I want to share it with you all. As someone who thrives in social settings, I love connecting with others through sports and outdoor activities. I am involved in several wonderful communities of backpackers, mountaineers, paragliding pilots, outdoor enthusiasts, and Search & Rescue teams. In my free time, I also enjoy playing various sports like badminton, table tennis, and football with young schoolchildren. It not only boosts my mood but also provides a fascinating glimpse into the thoughts of

Gen-Z and Gen-Alpha. In addition, I engage with a senior citizens' pensioner society, where retirees work together and find ways to give back to society. It is incredibly fulfilling to learn from their life journeys. I help them organize programs in rural areas to address social issues like drug addiction, dowry practices, female feticide and raising awareness on tree plantation, organic farming, and voting etc. One of these efforts led to the record planting of over 15,000 trees. Regularly interacting with individuals from both these extreme ends of the age spectrum is truly rewarding.

Apart from all these social activities, when I am on my own, I like to work out, do yoga, watch movies with family, hang out and gossip with friends in my free time.

(13) Finding balance is the key

It's easy to get sucked into the daily grind and become obsessed with achieving our goals, whether that means winning an Olympic medal or accomplishing something else. Sometimes the pressure builds up so much that we forget why we started in the first place. Probably because it was fun and you enjoyed and loved it. It is not solely about pushing you to the brink of exhaustion or constantly striving for a win. It's also about reconnecting with the reason you began, reframing your relationship with the task at hand—if that's possible. Try to find a way to rework your routine so that you can rediscover the enjoyment and fun that you may have lost along the way.

Sure success indeed requires discipline and hard work, but it is just as important to integrate that into your dynamic life in a way that keeps the task at hand enjoyable. In the process, you may be required to separate your self-worth from your performance. Temporarily stepping away from intense or high-pressure situations allows us to gain a fresh lens of perspectives look through. Remember the person you spend the most of your time in life is you only. So while it is essential to be kind to others, the person you should be the kindest to is yourself.

(14) Social media menace

"Happy pictures of unhappy people!"

Younger generations are growing up immersed in the world of Social media. This constant exposure raises the question of whether they project a kind of confidence that isn't truly their own—a confidence fashioned from narratives of catastrophic events they have read about or heard of, yet never genuinely experienced firsthand. Social media, whether it be Instagram or Facebook, is intrinsically intrusive and sensational, built entirely around the art of presentation. In contrast, what we actually feel is honestly more often than not quite contradictory and dichotomous to how we depict it to be on social media which is filled with *"happy pictures of unhappy people"*. This divergence represents a significant struggle that we have faced and are likely to continue facing, as long as we give social media this sort of impetus and allow it to shape our self-expression.

Of course, the time we decide to spend on social media is ultimately our own choice. However, based on my personal experiences with many young people, I have seen how this dynamic can become overwhelmingly catastrophic to deal with. The unfortunate reality is that these young minds—accustomed to having social media as an integral part of their daily lives—tend to mold themselves into versions they create specifically because these versions are deemed acceptable. In reality, honestly, we are more often than not quite different from the images we project online.

My advice to any young person navigating today's cultural and social climate is to remain true to yourself because authenticity is what truly matters. The content or persona you create today will lose its significance in a few years unless it is a genuine reflection of who you are. In essence, unless what you create is organic and imbued with depth and meaning, it is unlikely to endure over time.

(15) A healthy mind resides in a healthy body

There is a very beautiful Sanskrit verse which encapsulates the idea that every asset in life—be it wealth, friendships, marital bonds, or even a kingdom—can be reclaimed; yet the one possession that cannot ever be regained is your body. If I were to offer a single piece of advice to my younger self, it would undoubtedly be to prioritize health. Engage in regular workout sessions, participate in various sports or simply go for a run or a cycling session. Whenever I find myself feeling alone or getting some free time, I invariably put on my sports shoes and step out to engage in some or other form of physical activity. Also, I wake up every day at 5:00 AM and believe that when it comes to changing your life, there is nothing more powerful than a solid morning routine. These routines have yielded me immense benefits that I can clearly observe as I now enter my 30s. I feel exceptionally youthful and am in the best physical shape I have ever experienced, which is consistently validated by my health reports and checkups. Moreover, exercising triggers the release of endorphins—those feel-good hormones that are closely linked to a sense of happiness.

Even if you are not a professional athlete or a dedicated sportsperson, incorporating daily physical activity into your life remains essential—even after you secure employment with any institution. Making time for your body fosters a robust fitness culture. For instance, regularly visiting a badminton or tennis court to play a sport might not lead to groundbreaking achievements, but it ensures that you stay fit.

Additionally, the lessons learned on the playing field are invaluable. When you compete, you will experience victories as well as defeats and these experiences teach you that setbacks should never lead to demoralization. They show you that you must not be bogged down by losses, always have to maintain a positive outlook, take challenges in your stride, accept your mistakes and strive to improve in the next game and the next and so on.

(16) Mother Nature ki sharan

"Tread lightly. Breathe deeply. And appreciate
what lies in the outdoors beyond the playgrounds."

Too often our relationship with wild places has been described as the struggle of man versus nature, which is a flawed way of looking at the world. Instead of placing ourselves in opposition to other species, whether it be trees, insects, birds or animals, we should try to understand the vital connections that exist between human beings and other plants and creatures. Only then we will find inspiration and reassurance in places where nature has been untouched by man. We should approach forests, meadows, rivers and mountains with humility and reverence rather than trying to dominate these natural domains.

When it comes to spending a few days away from home, on a trek or a camping trip, we often speak about stepping out of our *"comfort zone"*. Yet, there is an inherent irony in that phrase because nobody should feel uncomfortable outdoors. Of course, sleeping under the stars or following a path that does not appear on a map is not an everyday experience for most people. Though anthropologists tell us that our ancestors once lived amidst nature, human beings have become burrowing creatures who now make their homes in elaborately constructed dens of concrete. We tend to feel more secure indoors.

However, when we do, occasionally, escape from the controlled, protected environments we have manufactured for ourselves, it allows us to make startling discoveries about the natural world and ourselves. Spending time in the outdoors can be a transformative experience. We develop life skills and how to apply them in different situations, confidence and team-building skills and to connect strongly with nature. These are not *"survival skills"*, as some might think, but instead an essential way of living and relearning our human instincts.

In the midst of life's challenges, nature offers a gentle refuge—a serene retreat where the heart can find solace and the mind can rediscover its strength. The rhythmic whisper of the wind through towering trees, the soft murmur of a hidden stream and the expansive canvas of a starlit sky remind us that beauty persists even in our darkest hours. The vibrant hues of a blooming garden, the delicate dance of sunlight on leaves, and the peaceful cadence of a flowing river all serve as nature's own symphony—a symphony that soothes our worries and whispers hope into our souls. Amid the natural world, each breath becomes a healing ritual, a moment to reconnect with our inner selves and embrace the simple wonders that abound.

Nature is more than just a backdrop to our lives; it is a living, breathing companion on our journey through hardship. It not only nurtures our spirit and lifts our mood but also instills in us a deep sense of gratitude for the present moment.

(17) The lowest point in life can be the start of a peak

"It is not the mountain in front of us but it is the mountain within ourselves that we climb. "

During one of my work trips to Sri Lanka, I was preparing to enjoy a relaxing weekend when, very unexpectedly, I encountered an opportunity to join a hiking expedition into the notorious Knuckles mountain ranges during the rainy season. I thought that it would be easier since I had some experience of hiking in the Himalayas. Our group consisted of twelve men and three women and I was the only foreigner among us. This was a self-sustained trip and upon noticing the organizers laboriously lifting tents and carrying cooking equipment, I immediately offered my assistance and shared the heavy load.

I had no idea what I had truly signed up for until leeches began making their way under my pants and shirt. The feeling was utterly disgusting as they sucked my blood and even concealed themselves in the most private areas. The relentless rainy and windy weather further compounded our difficulties, making it extremely challenging to even locate suitable spots for breaks. However, the organizers were a close-knit group of friends who seemed considerably experienced. They managed to find good locations for pitching our tents and prepared an amazing dal-rice dinner that lifted our spirits. We navigated extremely tough terrains and, at times, waded partly through small river streams in order to avoid the persistent leeches.

We spent the second night in vast, hollow caves where we gathered around a bonfire, sang, danced, talked and enjoyed late into the night. Overall, it turned out to be an adventure of a lifetime. Amid the super tough conditions, I experienced a remarkable sense of camaraderie and inclusiveness that deepened my love for the outdoors.

Thereafter to build expertise in the outdoors, I took a 4-week mountaineering course which had a big impact on my life. The parallels between mountaineering and life are fascinating. It shattered my perspective of what I can achieve, what I can endure, where my limits lie way more than I ever might have considered possible.

I have solo trekked to the Mount Everest Base Camp at an elevation of 17,598 feet, where I experienced firsthand the tough lives of the Sherpa clan. During that trek, I literally encountered both a lack of oxygen and a heightened appreciation for the value of life. As my gasps for oxygen become greater, the chaos in my head becomes quieter. It is astonishing what we can achieve when we allow ourselves the opportunity and take chances.

Also, I realized it is not the mountain in front of us but it is the mountain within ourselves that we climb. Often, the most formidable challenges are not those that tower before us in the physical world, but those that reside deep within our own hearts and minds. The mountain we truly climb is the one built of our inner doubts, fears and the scars of past defeats. Each step upward is a testament to our will to overcome. The journey, though arduous, gifts us with insights and strength that can redefine our very existence. So whenever you feel like hitting the lows in life, just remind yourself of the beautiful peak which you gonna climb now. Remember the mountain concept always!

(18) Search & Rescue

One of the biggest achievements in my life so far has been to save a life by performing CPR on a clinically dead person. Holding another person's life in your hands is an experience both intense and grounding. It taught me that even under intense pressure we have to trust in our abilities. That moment remains with me as a powerful reminder that we are often capable of far more than we realize. I am certified in advanced First Aid and First Responder and I remain committed to advancing my skills and preparedness, always ready to act decisively in moments of crisis. The honor I receive from these missions is not measured by accolades or any amount of money but by the simple, yet profound, act of giving someone a second chance to live.

Over the years, I voluntarily participated in many rescue operations and supported relief efforts. One of the intense ones was a night Search & Rescue at an altitude of 6000 meters amid -10°C temperatures in the Gangotri range of the Garhwal Himalayas, near the Indo-China border in Uttarakhand, India. Every such experience has deepened my understanding of the preciousness of life and taught me the deep meaning of resilience, the power of teamwork and the profound impact of united communities in critical times. Working alongside different teams, I learned how to think swiftly on my feet, make quick decisions under pressure and adapt to unpredictable situations—all while coordinating with diverse stakeholders to achieve a shared objective. I have also learned the indispensable truth that you must first rescue yourself to be able to rescue others. This self-preservation fortifies our ability to help those in need and to be in a position where you can help when things go wrong

I feel privileged undertaking multiple rescues at no cost. It's never about ego or recognition—just the simple belief that no one should be left behind. This journey has also served as a humbling reminder that the summit is always optional—what truly matters is getting home safely.

(19) Expectation and Comparison are the thieves of joy

Our distress often arises not from others but from our expectations of them. When we let go of expectations, no one can disturb us. A stranger on the street cannot trouble us because we expect nothing from them. However, we often feel disturbed by family or friends because of the expectations we place on them. This sentiment is beautifully captured in the following Sanskrit verse:

> *"He who harbors no expectations remains ever joyful; in every moment of life, his peace flows unceasingly."*

Low expectations can be a quiet gateway to lasting happiness. When we lower our demands, we release ourselves from the cycle of perpetual disappointment and instead embrace the simple beauties out there. This gentle shift in perspective allows us to appreciate small, unexpected moments that create space for genuine contentment and the natural flow of life.

Similarly, in a world brimming with achievements, possessions and milestones, it's all too easy to fall into the trap of comparing our journey to someone else's highlight reel. Feel lost and confused in life and feel like everyone has everything figured out but you. When we measure our lives against the vibrant tapestries of others, we lose sight of our own beauty. There is nothing to be gained from comparing your life to anyone else's. Each of us is a unique story, woven from our own experiences, dreams and challenges. When we shift our focus inward and honor our individual path, we begin to see that true happiness does not lie in external benchmarks but in the simple act of being. Embracing our own progress, no matter how small nurtures a deep sense of contentment and self-love. It frees us from the relentless pursuit of perfection and allows our inner light to shine.

In letting go of expectations and comparisons, we open ourselves to a life filled with gratitude and peace—a life where every moment is savored for its own worth. By celebrating our personal journey, we reclaim the joy that they so subtly steal and we find that happiness blossoms from within.

(20) Life is a journey

"kabhi dhoop kabhi chaanv "

I frequently compare life's journey to the experience of walking under a blazing sun on a sweltering day. At times, one stumbles upon the cool refuge of a tree's shade—a brief period where one can pause and relax. This resembles the transient nature of happiness; it is a fleeting delight that cannot last forever, for eventually, you must leave that comforting haven behind and press on with your journey. There are moments when the sun's intensity seems almost unbearable, yet relief can emerge unexpectedly in the form of drifting clouds or the joyful blessing of a sudden rain shower. What makes this analogy so fascinating is that we can never predict whether the upcoming stretch of our journey will be bathed in pleasant light or shrouded in hardship, nor can we foresee when the next burst of happiness will grace our path.

Do not be overwhelmed by beautiful things. The ripest fruit on the tree that dropped into your open palms can overwhelm you. A flood of sweetness can blur that true desire that once led you with clarity. Allow yourself the space to pause, to silence the myriad voices that compete for your attention. Rest beneath that generous tree of abundant gifts and select the nectar that your heart most earnestly calls for.

Do not fret over the tough phases in life. They are bound to come into everyone's life in one form or another. Life is, at its core, about weathering these tough periods, fighting them out and emerging stronger on the other side. But remember, if you can manage to face adversity with a smile, the entire journey is going to be a memorable one that not only enriches your life but also molds you into a better human being.

In today's results-driven world, everyone aspires to secure that coveted top spot. Many times in my life I, too, have experienced the crushing weight of pressure and the sting of insecurity. I have often found myself striving to protect my performance and reputation, burdened by the belief that I cannot afford to falter and must perform flawlessly each day. In this relentless pursuit of excellence, we often lose sight of the simple joy of truly living life to its fullest.

And that's the only real challenge we have, how to not complicate matters and not go away from the simple joy that life offers. Keeping that spark of excitement alive—even when things are not going your way—is the real test. Keep your head high and a big wide smile on your face.

A Letter To My Younger Self

Dear Younger Me,

As I complete my 20s journey, this is what I would say to my younger self. Live happily and once you stop fighting it, allow yourself to dive in completely. At first, it will suck. Most firsts always do. But you will absolutely love it by year almost two. Pick a morning playlist that sets the tone, light your incense and write your to-dos.

Simplify what you can, prioritize the things you want and strike out those you don't want to do. The anxiety of anticipation and the burden of procrastination are far worse than whatever it is you're avoiding. Life is much easier when you need not conform. Don't let it scare you that all the different versions of you can be true at once. You never had to choose a single version of yourself; every bit of you belongs exactly where you are.

Step out and make mistakes. Imbibe in your guts that it is absolutely fine and acceptable to make mistakes or blunders. It does not matter if you fall down, it is whether you get back up and how you choose to talk to yourself afterward that matters. The comeback is stronger than the setback. Sometimes no matter how hard you try, sometimes it isn't just meant to be. In the end, the whole life becomes an act of letting go as nothing is permanent.

Life is short. Time is flying fast. No replays, no rewinds. So romanticize the beauty of the present moment as it comes while you can. Chase real dopamine. The most profound art emerges from deep feeling, so please, never belittle your emotions, don't think yourself silly. It's simply not your job to make sense of everything —just focus on what is happening right now, not what will happen next.

Self-growth is about finding genuine peace in the uncertainty of *"I don't know yet"*. Control is a peculiar force; it exists because without it, life could be overwhelmingly chaotic and one of the best remedies for that chaos is laughter. Keep reading, writing and traveling. Stop endlessly talking about your plans, take decisive action and do what you know deep down you're meant to do. You are always just a few moments away from embarking on your journey and that's the way life unfolds. At first, it sucks, but eventually, as always, when you look behind, you are gonna love it. Never give up, in the end, it will all be worth it.

Dream big!

Epilogue

"The journey is the reward" There is no better person to vouch for this proverb than me.

As I reflect on the rich tapestry of my 20s, I am filled with a profound sense of gratitude for every twist and turn that has brought me to this moment. This memoir has been more than a recounting of events—it has been an honest exploration of life's unpredictable journey. Looking back, I see a decade of experiences that have shaped my understanding of happiness—not as a fixed destination, but as a series of fleeting yet profound moments. The friendships that anchored me, the mentors who guided me and of course the failures that tested me have all contributed to the person I am today.

Thank you for walking this path with me. May you continue to seek out strength and miracles in everyday life. I hope that these pages inspire you to cherish your own journey. Remember that every setback is an opportunity for growth and that the pursuit of happiness is an ongoing process—one enriched by love, laughter and the shared moments that make life so beautifully unpredictable.

So what does chasing happiness really mean?

Remember in our school days, we all heard a story that is still imbibed in me. It beautifully sums up the concept and the tensions behind it. "When I was five years old, my mother always told me that happiness is the key to life. When I went to school, they asked me what I wanted to be when I grew up. I wrote down *'happy'*. They told me I didn't understand the assignment and I told them they didn't understand life".

EPILOGUE

Author's Bio

Mr. Ankit Balwada is an entrepreneur and technology professional who is passionate about educating outdoor skills and environmental protection. He has extensive experience in developing and leading Experiential Outdoor Education programs around Interpersonal and environmental skills for school curriculum and adventure organizations. So far, these programs have benefitted over 1,000 individuals, ranging in age from 8 to 80 years.

Ankit is also an experienced First Responder, Mountaineer and Paragliding pilot. He is an avid traveler and has solo trekked to the Everest Base Camp (17598 ft) along with 3 high-altitude passes in the Nepal Himalayas. With a life motto of saving human lives, he actively leads and helps local authorities in organizing Search & Rescue operations and provides First Aid in disaster-prone and resource-constricted Himalayan regions.

He is an unshakable optimistic and believes in our ability to build a bright future together. *Chasing Happiness* is his debut non-fiction novel intended to bring about a positive change regarding mental health and happiness among youths in society.

You can reach out to him via Email at ankitbalwada7182@gmail.comand also follow his travel and life adventures on Instagram: **barefoot_dreamer_**